Every Note, a Lantern

Every Note, a Lantern

Poems by

Mary Katherine Creel

Cover design by Shay Culligan
Cover art by Jim Morgan

ISBN: 978-1-63980-541-9

Kelsay Books
502 South 1040 East, A-119
American Fork, Utah 84003
Kelsaybooks.com

For Kiki

Acknowledgments

Thank you to the following publications, where versions of these poems previously appeared:

Atticus Review: "Auras"

The Weekly Pause: "Before the Longest Night"

Contents

After the Hawk

A terrible marvel—
pile of plucked feathers
beneath the sugar maple.

No blood or bones, still
a gruesome reminder
this is what life gives us,

an unforgiving space
marked by beauty
and terror,

a garden of grief
we must tend
every season.

Wintering

The body is
a blue wood aster

with heart-shaped leaves
and nodding flowers—

shooting stars
in a wild space.

It's not the colony
holding the roadside bank

where the body feels
at home, but alone

beneath the dogwood
in a tangle of

blackberry canes
and Virginia creeper,

persisting amid
the harshness of winter.

Loss

The only fruit
from this womb—

dark clots
the size of wild plums

we once picked
from a tree
in your mother's yard.

It's too soon to know
if there was life,

or just decades
of loss

accumulating, still.

This Is Where Grief Leaves Us

In an empty house
where sadness sings

endlessly as a mockingbird,
flaunting white wing bars

to guard the absurdity
of bright red holly berries.

We acclimate to the familiar
darkness of winter,

ice-fogged windows
framing the slow

procession of a world
we cannot enter.

We give thanks
for the sustenance

of silence—
tiny embers lighting

this ancient cave,
the body.

Into the Dimming Daylight

Memory is a fragile thing,
solitary shape-shifter

rising from the leaf litter
like a magpie inkcap.

Short-lived, fruiting body,
by late morning, already

transforming its elongated
egg shape into a brown bell,

curling up along the lip
before pleated gills

deliquesce, send spores
into the dimming daylight.

The Chimney Swifts

Nighthawks make chase
in the dim half-light

cueing katydids
& crickets to sync with

the high-pitched chatter
of a gathering cloud.

In the old school parking lot,
watchers lose focus

trying to capture
with camera lenses

this seemingly infinite
nimbus, swirling

like snowflakes
in a globe some deity

keeps shaking, just so
we can marvel at

the elegance of swifts
as they drop, one by one,

into the mouth
of a stone tower.

The Heart Wants

To find promise
in the olive plumage

of a wintering kinglet,
the flash

of its striking ruby crown,
otherwise hidden.

Instead, it's a wren
that somehow found its way

into the heat pump,
ascending to heaven

with wings outstretched
and limp neck hung

in a metal grate,
its stocky body

impossibly suspended
above silver fan blades.

The heart wants to unsee
terrible things,

still, we hoard them
like acorns cached by

blue jays, germinating
and sustaining

a dark forest.

After So Many Days of Rain

Another mass shooting,
this time at a ballroom dance studio

on the cusp of the Lunar New Year.
I start believing

this is what we deserve—
a world clouded-over & without light.

I let the gray haze have its way,
darken every room, until the song

from a Carolina wren bubbles up,
cheer, cheer, cheer.

The Piano

For weeks, we didn't recognize
each other, even though
we slept in the same bed.

It wasn't the dark that hid
the winter dens of our bodies,
but the moonlit place on the floor

where the dog used to sleep.
We existed, but only in spirit,
because nothing we ate

fed us. You emerged first,
sturdier & more resilient,
recognized my inability

to keep treading water.
So you did the only thing
you could & gave me a piano.

Doubt

The hummingbird did not appear
when I prayed for a sign

that God exists.
I was still wintering,

oblivious to
the pollen-dusted stamens

and pistils popping off
all around me.

Later, as I hung
a newly filled feeder—

the sudden brush
of a fast-moving body,

sharp chirps and
the low hum

of tiny wings, beating.
From the branch

of a nearby poplar,
its ruby-sequined throat

flashes in short bursts
and long dashes,

signaling
look, here.

Auras

After a night of seizures & heat lightning,
the old dog fights sleep, frightened by
auras, I imagine, flicker behind her
copper eyes like a gas-blue flame.
I am also fighting sleep, watching her
pace the room like a drunk, pausing
every few minutes to tilt her head
& listen to apparitions. She leans
into me again, her body stiff, except
for one speckled ear, delicately folded
like an origami crane. Her white lashes
glow in the light of the television as
my own body hums. We sleep beneath
a cloud of worry, wait for the next storm.

A Prayer

I want to ask for nothing
even in the storm,

and by nothing, I mean,
the sun-warmed tidal pools

we waded through
on walks to Bird Island,

sting of sand and salt,
brackish mudflats

and loggerhead tracks,
hundreds of red fiddler crabs

waving giant claws.
This is a prayer, after all,

for a burrow hidden
in marsh grass,

refuge from a life
spent mostly in flight.

Before the Longest Night

Take inventory of what is becoming—
ruffled buds on bony maple branches,

moth cocoons woven from
oak silk and last season's leaves.

Pocket rose quartz, pyrite
and downy woodpecker feathers,

leave an offering of coneflower seeds
for chickadees and finches, listen

for the hum of bees—winter queens
and masons tunneling in.

Make a wild space for burrows
and dens, let your shadow

catch fire on the wall at dusk,
flare around the edges

and sear a charcoal-smudged silhouette
to remember these dark hours.

Rescued

Still as a package
on the front steps—

a hermit thrush with
russet wings tucked

and white-ringed eyes
too dark to decipher

fear or connection
during a slow-motion

rescue. You remember
her haunting song

for days after she flies
from the yellow bells

into the fog, and find
your way back.

The Altar

I give my grief
to the cypress blown down
by a winter storm,
wood chips like ashes,
the staccato of logs
tossed onto a pile
by the rusted burn
barrel—a makeshift altar
to honor what gave us
the melodic song
of a wood thrush that one
summer, bark ribbons
curled in the mouths
of mothers, giant leopard
moths waiting out the day,
a thousand silhouettes
at sunset, and the ghost
of an orange and white cat
napping beneath
sweeping branches.

Stay

If you leave now, you will miss
the way morning light falls
across the floor beneath
the piano bench, the way
windows frame bare branches
and blooms bent by bees
too cold to gather nectar.

You will not be here to see
the ocean of oak leaves
that fell overnight, blanketing
our labors from summer,
or frost that came too early,
glinting like diamonds on
the old Volkswagen.

You will miss finding
that mysterious feather
and the river rock imprinted
with blue-gray striations
in the shape of a labyrinth,
miss the sleek black cat
you nicknamed *Morpheus*
sunning in the garden,
a pair of chickadees scouting
the empty bluebird house,
that feeling of purpose
when we give
shelter in the long winter.

Every Note, a Lantern

By noon, windshield ice crystals
have vanished, returned to vapor.

What will I return to? Warmth of
morning sun like a womb,

wood thrush song, a memory of
being held by water. When I vanish,

what will I miss? Pale blue spots
on a giant leopard moth,

a squinting tabby, soft & round
as a buddha, sunning beneath

the tulip poplar, hearing my love laugh
in another room, the way he coos

to the dogs before leaving for work,
& later, afternoon sun triangles

gilding the piano, transposing
winter's return

to the light; every note, a lantern.

Welcome, Grief

Let it come together
and scatter

like the flock of starlings
circling

a winter sky
with cotton-batting clouds.

Let it roost
and make a ruckus

in the woods across the street
where red oaks

hold on
to shuddering leaves.

Watching the Old Dog Sleep

More often, I find myself watching
for the rise and fall of breath
while she sleeps on her side,
legs folded like a jackknife
and one black ear draping the edge
of the couch like a felt triangle,
speckled at the tip. I give thanks for
moments of stillness, any semblance
of contentment, even though I miss
the way she used to jump up and
throw her paws around my waist,
dance with me and make the record
skip. Now she clings to me for
different reasons, following my
footsteps as if they were a heatmap
in this new world, where every sense
is altered by seizure medication
and the tumor in her brain. I trace
the white stripe along her head
and neck, jagged as bark scarred
by lightning, forgive her grumbling.

Sorrow Does Not Live Here

In the pink plumes
of muhly grasses—

electric capillaries
pulsing with a memoir

of dawn. A shift in
perspective

and spikelets
flare magenta,

rise up from a crown
of leaf ribbons

curled with the edge
of a scissor blade.

Happiness

Just bloomed & already
closing by mid-morning—

a saffron-yellow star, born
on the vine from a place

we once tended together.
This is how happiness

makes an appearance,
a volunteer's first flower

beaming beside ragged
snail-scraped leaves.

After so many lanterns
doused and left to soften

in our forgotten garden,
a single seed disrupts

this season of grief.

This Morning, a Gift

Wrapped in
the gauze of dawn

soft muzzle
    to damp cheek

bristle of whiskers
from a little wolf

    leaning in
to fuse fur with ribs

as if to keep me
from   drifting.

If the Heart Needs Hope

Let it be found
in an ordinary thing—

the slender teardrop
of a daffodil

just before it blooms,
white wood violet,

bittercress and bird's eye
speedwell, too,

a tulip tree's velvet buds,
and chorus frogs

calling from the stream
behind the house

like hundreds of fingertips
raking across

teeth on
a plastic comb.

This Garden We've Dreamed

After pounding rain, I try to prop
the milkweed back up, brush
away clumps of mulch and
red clay from baby Joe Pye
weed, planted just yesterday.

My clothes are soaked
from this persistent drizzle,
so I go inside where you
assure me the plants will right
themselves when the sun returns.

What does it mean, this garden
we've dreamed—one minute,
alive and bright with winged things,
the next, sodden and sad,
overcome by flood water?

Later, the lemon-yellow promise
of a cloudless sulphur
on a newly opened purple aster,
and eggs like citrine beads
on the swamp milkweed.

While the Neighbor Is in Jail

I think of writing a letter to tell him
about the pair of Eastern phoebes

that made a mud cup nest under
his deck, how they perch on the railing

in late afternoon, skim the yard
for crane flies like feathered

bombers. Would he find it amusing,
the time I looked up while walking

the dog and saw the question mark
of a cat's tail bob past windows

on the landing, just as the string of
party lights flickered on at dusk?

He would be happy to know,
the neighbor on the hill offered

to mow his grass and pick up limbs
so the house looks lived in,

and the other neighbor brings
her great granddaughter

when she comes by after work
to feed his three cats,

remembering to roll the trash bins
to the curb every Monday.

It's true, the world goes on
without us, and grass grows back,

covering the scorched earth
where fire burned out of control.

Salvation

Scooped from the blue
water bowl left for the dogs,

a carpenter bee recovers
in my cupped palm.

I once read that a bee
can hold its breath for

five minutes, but this one
is wetter than a river otter

and so much smaller.
I trust she won't sting

and give her time
to groom away water

weighing
cellophane wings.

Her abdomen pulses
like a tiny heart.

There is no signal
to know she is ready,

just a quick lift
and drunken spiral,

up and
over the house.

Praise

For the giant leopard moth
grounded on the front steps,

the way it crawls from leaf
to palm and pointer finger,

clasping on with black legs
wiry as brush bristles.

Praise for its orange-and-
blue-striped abdomen,

the wonder of something
as small as your thumb

having such a presence,
as if the universe itself

was emanating from
its powder-white wings

and feathered antennae
bending toward you.

Rush

Most days, I don't know
what prayer is, or if

I am doing it right,
but I can tell you

a flock of goldfinches
is called a charm.

You could also call
this yellow spectacle

a rush or trembling,
which is how it felt

to pause and watch
a dozen or more

dip and splash in
the copper bird bath.

I have prayed for
peace, to feel it

even in the midst
of chaos,

and isn't this it—
the heart open as

a field sunflower
with petals like gold

feathers, radiating
from its dark center?

In the Church of a Weeping Cherry

After a storm, the miracle
of pale pink flowers,

tissue-paper lanterns
glimmering with honey

light. We seek shelter
in this humming

cathedral, held together
by cascading branches

and hundreds of
cellophane wings

glinting. The gloss
of promise overwhelms,

even in winter's false
spring—a feast for bees

already heavy
with pollen baskets.

A chipping sparrow
makes a trilling entrance,

tilts its copper crown;
together, we listen.

How to Sew Yourself Into the Earth

In the shade of
a live oak,

lie on your back
with arms

outstretched,
let spider silk

spool around thighs
& hips, held by

a ground-hugging
colony of wild

strawberry, sending
runners to loop

limbs & weave you in
a cocoon of

velvet tendrils
& white flowers.

About the Author

Mary Katherine Creel lives in the foothills of the Blue Ridge Mountains, where she has worked as a journalist and counselor to children and families. A Pushcart Prize nominee, she is author of the poetry chapbook *when fire injures, it leaves a distinctive wound* (dancing girl press) and *tunneling in,* a handmade, limited-edition book of micro-poems written during the pandemic. Recent poems have appeared in *Salvation South, Atticus Review, Humana Obscura, kerning, The Weekly Pause,* and *otata.* She also writes the Substack publication *a small spectacle,* featuring nature-inspired poems and short essays about finding gratitude, healing, and connection.

www.ingramcontent.com/pod-product-compliance
Lightning Source LLC
Chambersburg PA
CBHW070907100426
42737CB00047B/2976